I0475489

Bitcoin Profits Crash Course

• Learn How to Make Money With Bitcoin in 7 Days or Less! • The Ultimate Guide to Bitcoin Mining, Investing and Trading •

By Frank Richmond

Copyright © 2021. All rights reserved. No part of this book may be reproduced or transmitted in any form or any means, electronic or mechanical, including photocopying, recording or by any information storage and retrieval system, without the written permission of the author.

Disclaimer

Please note that the information contained within this document is for educational purposes only. Every attempt has been made to provide accurate, up to date, and reliably complete information. No warranties of any kind are expressed or implied. Readers acknowledge that the author is not engaging in the rendering of legal, financial or professional advice. The content of this book has been derived from various sources. Please consult a licensed professional before attempting any techniques outlined in this book.

Table of Contents

What Exactly is Bitcoin?

In a world of emails, online shopping and social media, Bitcoin was almost an inevitability. What all the many complicated elements of this system boil down to is a digital money environment, allowing units of currency to be stored and transmitted throughout the network to its users.

It's one of a few different cryptocurrencies out there – more about that later – but probably the one that most people you ask will already have heard of thanks to the dramatic rises and falls in its prices over recent weeks and months. Even so, you'll likely find that the number of people who are informed about Bitcoin and its peers is still incredibly low – this is a technology that is very much in its infancy and, at least in terms of the mainstream audience, will be for quite some time.

Despite that fact, a lot of early uptakers believe that it will eventually become the primary economic system on the planet, ultimately replacing the banks and government systems we have in place today. If that bold claim does contain more than a kernel of truth, it's probably going to be a long while before it happens, but there is a certain amount of sense behind the argument. So let's start from the very beginning and take a look at how we got where we are today...

The Evolution of Currency

Currency has been around almost as long as people have, at least in our civilized form; it refers to the specific "thing" that one person has used at a certain point in our history to transfer value to another person. Back in the mists of time, this was considerably simpler, because most populations worked on a barter system, so the currency in a particular community could at that time probably have been defined through a weird and wonderful mixture of sheep and cows, eggs and cheese or services such as construction.

Villager One needed a fence built, so they gave Villager Two, the local building expert, a week's supply of milk to get it done. Both villagers were happy because they had given what they could afford to give and received what they needed in return.

It didn't take long for these big brains of ours to figure out that there were flaws in the accepted system. If you wanted to head to the market to find some carrots for your stew and maybe a new rooster, you didn't really want to drag your cow herd behind you so you could get it done.

Some never-to-be-identified genius or geniuses came up with the idea of using representative units instead – shells, beads, bones or other items that could be handed over to the owner of that rooster as an "IOU" of sorts. The recipient could then trade those units in for items or services themselves, which the next person could trade in for the items and services they needed, and so on and so on as the idea of money was born.

Money eventually became the coins and paper we are still familiar with today and for hundreds of years this was carried around in a person's wallet, guaranteed by their country's financial system and used to buy whatever goods and services the person needed.

Then, of course, came the beginnings of the technological revolution and we replaced that paper and coinage with credit and debit cards, a much easier and less cumbersome way to access your available funds wherever you go. This was the twinkle in the father's eye for Bitcoin and its fellow cryptocurrencies, which aim to take the next inevitable step in this very long human journey by removing money from the equation almost entirely and trading currency completely online.

The Birth of Cryptocurrencies

A cryptocurrency is any digital currency that uses cryptography to make it secure. You might be wondering what makes using a currency like Bitcoin any different to brandishing your credit card at the gas station and what thus sets cryptocurrencies apart from any other currency we already use.

Simply put, cryptocurrencies are not governed by any central authority. There is no Federal Reserve or Bank of England, no government controlled mint creating coins and pieces of paper. They are neither made by nor controlled by any entity, which means they cannot be manipulated by any single individual or agency.

A cryptocurrency is a closed and perfect system all of its own, completely organic in its use and creation. These systems are so secure and hidden from interference that it is extremely difficult for a government to even find out who was responsible for an individual transaction that catches its eye.

If the thought has now crossed your mind that this can't possibly be popular with the world's governments, you would be right. Individual countries have historically manipulated their own currencies to keep the economy stable but, with cryptocurrencies, they relinquish that control entirely.

Not to mention that, yes, the sinister side of cryptocurrencies does exist. Because of the anonymity and security, currencies such as Bitcoin have been used since they were first launched into the public sphere by people and organizations with unfortunate intentions. They can be utilized for money laundering, for example, or to evade taxes – even illegal transactions.

However, the world is slowly coming around to the idea of digital finance and you'll find that, these days, quite a few banks have begun to make use of the technology themselves. The flaws that allow sinister transactions to take place shouldn't be overlooked, but cryptocurrencies also have some important advantages to offer. We'll come back to that later.

Financial Disaster and the Beginnings of Bitcoin

In many ways, Bitcoin arrived as a solution to the flaws in the existing system. You may recall, back in the first decade of the new millennium, that an economic crisis in America was affecting the world as a whole.

The checks and balances that should have kept the crisis from deepening as dramatically as it did had failed along the way. The banks in the USA had begun to give out loans that were more risky than usual with the idea of attracting new customers – but, as they probably should have expected, this actually led to a lot of people who couldn't afford that loan in the first place finding themselves defaulting on their payments.

The banks were using that money to invest – and not all of those investments paid off. Combined with the loss from the defaulted payments, this eventually led to a number of financial institutions going bankrupt, taking their customers' savings down with them. The government attempted a bailout, but this of course used public money that had been paid in taxes, which understandably caused widespread discontent.

The knock-on effects caused ripples all around the world because America represents one of the largest economies in modern existence. As the crisis rolled on, it began to shine a light on the big problems associated with centralized currencies.

One of the most important things that came to light during the crisis was that the system doesn't favor the average, everyday person. Quite the opposite, in fact.

A government spends money gathered from taxes for developing the country but, in some cases, must spend more than it actually has available.

When this happens, a centralized currency has the advantage of being able to ask its central bank to print more money and make it available to the public. There are no limits on the amount of money that a government can print.

This does help to pump more cash into the economy, but it also has the side effect of decreasing the value of the money that was already there. Combine this with the utter loss of trust in banks that came from the bankruptcies and personal losses, and the heartbreak people suffered as a result, and you have an environment in which an alternative is always going to look promising.

What Made Bitcoin Different?

In 2008, a paper was released called "Bitcoin: A Peer to Peer Electronic Cash System" by a person writing under the alias of Satoshi Nakamoto. It wasn't a completely new idea; in fact, Nakamoto had taken several inventions already in existence, such as HashCash, and used them to create a financial system that would no longer rely on any central authority for its operations.

At its heart was a brand new idea: the proof-of-work algorithm, holding global "elections" every ten minutes that allowed the network as a whole to reach a consensus about the transactions happening across it. This sidestepped the issue of double spend that had plagued early versions of cryptocurrencies (in which the system could be manipulated to spend the same money twice before anyone noticed) along with disadvantages such as the need to use a national currency as a backing or, alternatively, precious metals.

Bitcoin also solved the problem of unlimited currency by setting a limit on the maximum number of coins that could ever be in circulation and also on the rate at which new ones can be produced. This is hard wired into the system's code and cannot be violated and any user can view the code to verify it.

What this achieved was to ensure that the value of a single bitcoin is only affected by supply and demand within the marketplace and cannot be artificially manipulated. There is no government changing the value of the currency to influence the economy – it will only ever change in value according to its own merits and drawbacks.

Another big selling point for this brand new financial system was that it removed the third party from every equation. Traditionally, when a person has placed their money with a bank for storage, the bank has then had free rein to use that money how it pleases while it has hold of it.

In other words, banks make their profits by using a customer's cash to make investments. Most of the time, that's not something a customer would even think about or notice, but the financial crisis sadly made a lot of people all too aware of the potential risks.

With Bitcoin, customers could suddenly transact directly with one another using their digital accounts for storage and their digital wallets for payments. Again, the coding for these designs was made public so that it could be reviewed by anyone wishing to make sure of its security.

The First Bitcoins

The Bitcoin network was launched in 2009 from the fruits of Nakamoto's work, revised along its journey by numerous other programmers. Having decided that there will only ever be a certain number of bitcoins in existence, it became necessary to decide next how quickly they would be made – and who would get them.

Entirely at random, the number of bitcoins released was set at 50 every ten minutes. It was also decided, again entirely randomly, that this number would halve every four years. This was done as an incentive for those who took a chance on Bitcoin in its early days.

To answer the question of who would receive the bitcoins, the system was opened to miners. These people – or, rather, the computers belonging to these people – support the system by creating proofs of transfer to verify and record all the transactions that would be taking place. A bank does this too, recording everything you do with your money and keeping your balance correct, but Bitcoin doesn't have the need for a centralized bank for this purpose.

And so, instead, computers become the source of validation for every transaction you make. These computers save the data on the database after verifying them – and any computer can do it, as long as it is running the software provided by Bitcoin. Those early uptakers who offered their computers were dubbed miners and they were rewarded with freshly minted bitcoins. The more computational power a person could offer, the more they were rewarded.

The Sudden Rise of Bitcoin

In late 2017, the price of Bitcoin began to rise dramatically and the world began to take notice. Smelling the next get rich scheme coming a mile away, the media and financial experts began to pay much more attention to what had previously been a fairly obscure technology.

The reasoning behind Bitcoin had always been attractive and its vision of the future was tempting, but there was a drawback: not many vendors and companies actually accepted it. That, of course, meant that there weren't very many places on the planet to spend your bitcoins once you had earned them.

Over time, more merchants did start to accept bitcoins and more people began to take notice. However, the number of bitcoins in existence was, by design, growing more slowly than the number of people who were buying into the system, which meant that the price started to go up. From a fraction of a dollar, a single bitcoin was suddenly worth thousands of dollars.

Nakamoto withdrew from the public eye in 2011 and left Bitcoin's network to a group of volunteers. This didn't particularly matter and was done deliberately to prove that Nakamoto at no time had had any control over the system because it is based on mathematical principles and the consensus of participants.

It stands alone, continuing its work without interference from any person or government and – and, because of that fact, is likely to attract more and more interest as time goes by.

And Now for the Jargon...

Like every other topic of human invention, cryptocurrencies come with their very own terms, words and phrases. Before we dive into your introduction to them, let's familiarize you with that jargon so you feel more comfortable reading about it later on. The common terms you'll encounter in this book and beyond include:

- Address: The string of letters and numbers to which a cryptocurrency can be sent, much like an email address in purpose only much more random in its structure.
- Bip: This stands for Bitcoin Improvement Proposals made by members of the community.
- Bit: A single unit that can be combined to make a bitcoin. One bitcoin equals one million bits.
- Bitcoin: This can refer to the software, the network or the currency unit itself.
- Block: A collection of transactions using Bitcoin that have taken place during a set period of time, most usually ten minutes.
- Blockchain: A record of every Bitcoin transaction that has ever happened.

- BTC: The abbreviation used for the bitcoin currency.
- Chargeback: Reversing a payment or transfer after it has been authorized – sometimes used for fraudulent purposes.
- Coinbase: The input script for a transaction that generates new bitcoins, or a name for the transaction itself.
- Cold wallet: A wallet that is not connected to the internet and is therefore in cold storage. If the keys have been written down or printed out, it is often referred to as a paper wallet.
- Confirmations: A transaction is confirmed once it has been included in a block on the block chain. This needs to happen three times for coinbase to consider it is a final transaction.
- Cosigner: A person or entity who has some control over a Bitcoin wallet.
- Cryptocurrency: A type of money that does not use a central bank, but instead utilizes cryptography for its existence and to perform transactions.
- Cryptography: A mathematical method of securing information.
- Decentralized: Bitcoin is considered to be this kind of network because there is no central

authority or controller – it is not under the auspices of any company or government.

- Distributed network: This kind of network is designed so that participants must connect to one another directly, without a central server.
- Double spending: This term refers to a user managing to spend the same money more than once and is protected against with verifications on the blockchain.
- ECDSA: Elliptic Curve Digital Signature Algorithm, the algorithm used to ensure only the real owner can spend their funds.
- Encryption: This makes use of cryptography to encode a message in a way that only allows the person it was sent to to read it.
- Hash: The unique identifier associated with a Bitcoin transaction or the mathematical function used by Bitcoin miners to make the network more secure.
- Hot wallet: A wallet connected to the internet and therefore ready for use.
- Ledger: A log book that contains the transactions and balances of an account.
- M of N: M stands for signatures and N stands for cosigners. M of N is thus the number of cosigners who must sign for a multi-signature transaction to occur. For example, "4 of 5"

would mean that four of the cosigners must provide signatures.

- Miner: A computer or group of computers that adds transactions to blocks and verify the ones created by other computers. Miners are paid in bitcoins for their efforts and collect transaction fees.
- Multi-signature: Some transactions can only be completed with signatures from more than one individual.
- Node: A participant in the Bitcoin network.
- Open source: A software project with code that is available to the public and can be distributed freely.
- Peer to peer: In this network type, participants do not communicate through a central server but directly to one another.
- Private key: The string of letters and digits associated with a Bitcoin address that can be used to spend bitcoins.
- Public key: A string of letters and digits derived from a private key and used to receive bitcoins.
- Signature: Proof within a transaction that approval has been given by the owner of the private key.

- Transaction: One entry in the blockchain, representing a single transfer or set of transfers of bitcoins from one address to another address.
- Transaction fee: This is the fee collected by miners to encourage them to add that transaction to the block.
- Wallet: A collection of private keys that can be used to spend bitcoins.

This list is long, but only just scratches the surface of the terminology you're about to immerse yourself in. It'll give you a head start on understanding cryptocurrencies and entering the world of Bitcoin. You can refer back to it while you are reading if you need to remind yourself what a particular term means.

The Myths and Mysteries of Cryptocurrencies

As with most unfamiliar ideas, Bitcoin and its fellow cryptocurrencies have been plagued by myths and misconceptions since the very beginning. When mankind once saw open ocean as far as the eye could see, we did, after all, assume that there be monsters.

Many people are hesitant about diving into the world of cryptocurrencies precisely because of the myths that have bubbled up around them. To lay your concerns to rest before you think about joining the fray, let's debunk some of those false thoughts before they infect you with unnecessary fears:

- "Access to Bitcoins will run out eventually and the currency will deflate because there is a finite supply" – Yes, it is true that a limit was set on how many bitcoins could be put into circulation. As discussed, this was done with the best of intentions, to prevent the kind of devaluation that plagues traditional fiat currencies. The protocol is expected to create 21 million units over the next century, but it can be amended – as long as there is consensus from the community. If a majority of participants votes to make a change, as it did in the past with an update on how to specify payment conditions, that total can change. At the moment, it appears that the community is adamant in its defense of the designated limit, but that too could change in the future. Other digital currencies, now and in the days to come, may do away with the limits altogether.

- "Bitcoins aren't actually worth anything" – To answer this one, you first have to question if gold is worth anything. When the first piece of gold was dug out of the ground, did it come with a price tag attached? No, it became valuable because we decided it was valuable, just as we once decided that a week's worth of milk was of equal value to the building of a fence around our property. Currency as a whole has never really been backed by anything other than the consensus of its users, and Bitcoin is no different in that regard. As an example of how little this differs to other modern currencies, the US dollar was once figured according to the price of gold, but this practice was ended all the way back in 1933. Since then, just like Bitcoin, it hasn't been backed by anything much at all.

- "Eventually we won't need credit cards any more" – Possibly, yes, but that's a long way off. At the moment, Bitcoin is limited in the number of transactions it can handle, there is a delay before those transactions take effect and the associated fees are generally too high for regular commerce, depending on demand. Think of Bitcoin more as a reserve, where you can store value as with buying gold, than as a regular form of payment.

- "The anonymity will make Bitcoin a haven for criminals" – Bitcoin was founded on the idea that its users would have the protection of privacy, because each transaction uses pseudonyms instead of real names. This led to the suspicion that anonymity would breed a user base with less than pure intentions – money launderers, for instance, knowing that their crimes cannot be traced back to them through the currency. Obviously, this would be preferable to using a financial institution where your personal details are required to open an account. In fact, in the early days, it is true that Bitcoin was used by criminals including an underground drug market known as the "Silk Road". However, the human race is notorious for solving problems as they crop up and Bitcoin is no exception. Analysts have developed techniques through which they can study patterns in the blockchain and use them to link pseudonyms together – law enforcement agencies are already making use of this. So while, yes, there is anonymity built into the system, it is still possible to identify wrongdoers when necessary and true anonymity is still only really possible through using paper cash.

- "The law can't touch Bitcoin users" – Following on from the last myth, many people have assumed that a lack of a centralized authority means there is a lack of law enforcement capability. While it's true that government moves slowly and sometimes takes a while to catch up with new technology, it almost always does. Slowly but surely, states and countries are beginning to introduce their own laws on the use of cryptocurrencies and bitcoin exchanges are generally complying with "know your customer" laws meant to discourage money laundering. Even the IRS regards it as a taxable property these days.

- **"Governments are going to shut Bitcoin down eventually"** – While some of them would probably like to do this, that doesn't mean they can. The beauty of Bitcoin in the first place is that it is decentralized and has no "leader" at the top, which means there is nobody to arrest and prosecute and nobody to push the off switch. Shutting it down would, in fact, be a Herculean task that would involve shutting down the entire infrastructure across the internet.

- **"It's costly to the environment to run Bitcoin"** – All those miners around the world, each running computers with special hardware chips, use up a lot of electricity. Environmental campaigners have complained that this must add up to an extreme amount of electricity use, which could have a worrying impact in the long run. However, it's safe to say that regular currencies also have an impact on the environment. The lights need to stay on, computers are still used for transactions and every employee must travel back and forth to work and be given access to facilities that require power to run. The miners keep the system secure and this does require energy, but it's probable that this issue, too, will be solved as the technology matures.

- "It's really easy to hack a cryptocurrency" – This one does have a basis in truth, in that early cryptocurrencies were relatively easy to attack. Over time, however, security has continued to improve. The blockchain for Bitcoin, at time of writing this book, had never been hacked in its history and was Bitcoin was considered to be unbreakable for the forseeable future.

- "It's just a really big Ponzi scheme" – A Ponzi scheme is defined as an investment scam that promises high rates of return in exchange for very little risk to its investors. Nakamoto at no point made such a claim to his potential customers and the rise of Bitcoin was caused by speculators, not Bitcoin's actions. However, be wary of any unassociated group that makes a claim of this nature involving cryptocurrencies. Bitcoin, just like anything else, is vulnerable to the desires of unscrupulous humans.

- "Bitcoin is already dead" – You hear this one regularly, when the value of the cryptocurrency drops temporarily. Actually, there are more transactions taking place on the network every day than ever before and it's a technology that is unlikely to go away any time soon.

The Common Cryptocurrencies You'll Meet

This is a book about Bitcoin, so for the most part we have been and will be focusing on that specific cryptocurrency. But to provide yourself with a full education on this new technology, it's wise to be aware that Bitcoin is far from alone in the marketplace.

It may be the most famous and it may have been the focus of most reports on cryptocurrencies in the recent past thanks to the excitement of its ever-rising price, but pretty much anyone can actually invent a cryptocurrency, should they so desire. As you can imagine, that makes some of them more worthy of attention than others.

The big names in current cryptocurrency that you will want to watch out for include:

- Bitcoin – Still the big name in cryptocurrencies, this is the one that springs to mind for most people when one mentions that word. It is, in fact, so synonymous with the technology that most other cryptocurrencies are referred to as "altcoins" because they are an alternative to Bitcoin. For this reason, it's a

29

good idea to start with Bitcoin when you are looking to get involved with cryptocurrencies, even if you decide to eventually branch out.

- Ripple – This currency is also designed to be an open payment network, allowing users to transfer currency to others. It works in a very similar way to Bitcoin with the purpose of connecting payment systems used by different people. This bypasses the problems of companies using different systems and makes sure that funds can be transferred efficiently no matter where and to whom they are going. However, be aware that this cryptocurrency is an anomaly in that it is actually centralized – it is controlled by a consortium of banks, mostly in Japan, which means you lose a certain amount if you transfer some currencies.

- Litecoin – Though functionally very similar to Bitcoin, this currency can be processed significantly faster because a customer does not need to wait for a miner to verify the transaction. It can therefore be used to make online payments very quickly.

- Monero – The big focus of this currency is privacy. Monero is known for being secure and untraceable, which makes it popular in countries where citizens can be punished for their actions if they are perceived as anti government. The system achieves this by introducing multiple keys into a transaction.

- Etherium – Also known as Ether, this currency differs from Bitcoin largely in its approach to the source code. It offers Smart Contracts, which allow people to code and enact contract terms without a third party's assistance, and therefore can solve the problem of legal contracts being handled online. A Smart Contract takes action automatically once the conditions that were agreed on are met and will follow the terms of the agreement precisely. There are also very few limits placed on the code's processing ability, which allows developers to dream up almost endless application possibilities.

- Factom – This system is known primarily for being an unbreachable record of data. It uses a blockchain to maintain records and document data in a way that cannot be changed in any way and then store this on a decentralized network that is almost invulnerable to tampering.

- Dash – This currency is used for intraday trading but is also useful for everyday spending opportunities and is looking to become to go-to currency for quick payments and money transfers. Its Dash Evolution project is touted as the best available alternative to PayPal, for example.

- Golem – Through this system, you can "rent out" your computer's processing power to other people, allowing machines located in different places to work together on a project. Your computer could therefore be used for anything from data analysis to scientific research while hooked up to the Golem system.

- Zeash – Also known for its anonymity, this system uses zero knowledge proofs to create more privacy.

Not every currency is reliable. A notorious cryptocurrency, for example, is Dogecoin, which was invented purely as a joke and nobody expected that a meme of a dog's face would ever circulate. It has no value and is almost never used.

Because there are hundreds of cryptocurrencies out there, it's a daunting world for a beginner. For this reason, it's best to place your focus in a single area – and Bitcoin remains the best option for that focus at this time. Keep an eye on other currencies, by all means, but learn the tricks of the trade with the biggest name in the business.

More About the Blockchain

The technology that underpins the entire cryptocurrency system is the blockchain. We've mentioned its existence already but, as a potential investor, it's the one part of the system you should have a strong understanding of as you make your preparations to invest.

The blockchain goes all the way back to the 1980s, when home computing was still very much in its infancy. At that time, a programmer was already receiving the dreaded spam emails and was growing impatient with them clogging up his inbox.

What he developed in an attempt to stop that spam was a "proof of work" model: a math problem that gets more and more difficult the more times it is asked to verify details at one time. A single email was fine, even the computers of that time could handle the equation. They could not, however, handle the thousands of solutions that would be needed to send out a piece of spam.

Decades passed, however, before this proof of work model saw any real use. It wasn't put forward on a large scale until 2008, when programmers realized that it could potentially be used to underpin a new type of currency that would be free from the usual framework of the financial system. The idea was discussed on an online forum, where it was seen by Satoshi Nakamoto.

Nakamoto, as you may already have guessed, saw more potential in the idea than his fellow users. He used it to design his new technology for blockchain and thus the bitcoin was born, and many other programmers saw the possibilities in his ideas and joined him.

The blockchain itself is a database that is decentralized (i.e. is located on many different machines at one time, rather than a central server) and acts as the ledger for Bitcoin's financial transactions. Its design and security make it easy for authorized users to access it, but tough for unauthorized users to do the same.

Each individual block in the chain contains unique information about a transaction as well as information that designates its place inside the chain. Every time a new block is added, its information is verified and then shared with all the other nodes, which seek that new information without needing to be told to do so. The block is also given a time stamp, making it easy to see when that transaction took place.

As a user, you will be filling up your own block when you make a transaction, until that block is filled and will be added to the chain to become part of the permanent record, linking with every other block that belongs to you. Each block is secure and can contain a huge amount of data that isn't limited to a transaction's price tag – it can also contain, for example, digital rights information, the title to a property and much more.

Every user has their own chain full of their own transactions, but those individual blocks will also become part of the overall blockchain to keep them safe. This keeps the system both secure and transparent.

However, to make sure that other users can't take advantage of this transparency to steal the information inside your blocks, codes are added to keep it safe from hackers. Others can see your transactions, but what's actually going on is hidden by these hashes. The miners are responsible for adding these codes and are paid for doing so successfully.

In terms of security measures, the blockchain is all about defense. It has no offensive options when it is threatened, but relies on high levels of defense to keep itself safe. For instance, transactions must be verified before they can be added to the chain, which means that any malevolent blocks can and will be picked up instantly and automatically and thrown out before they can enter and infect the chain. The data of a single block needs to line up with at least half of all the other nodes before it can be added.

Could a hacker fake the information that would get it past the system's checks? In theory, yes, but not yet. At the moment, the resources and costs associated with such a task are beyond the reach of hackers and the gains would not be worth the price even if they could.

The blockchain, to the uninitiated, seems a little like space magic, but it's actually an elegant system that's easy to understand once you know how it works. This technology is the basis of everything that happens with Bitcoin and its fellow cryptocurrencies and is the system upon which your investments will always be made.

The Pros and Cons of Bitcoin

With a little more understanding of Bitcoin under your belt, both the philosophical reasons for its birth and the way that this currency works, you may be beginning to wonder whether it's the right investment for you. Perhaps the volatility of Bitcoin is worrying you, as its popularity and novelty tend to combine into headlines about crashes and dire times.

So let's take a closer look at this currency and its pros and cons, both as an entity that exists and a potential investment for you:

Pros

- Bitcoin allows you to send or receive money from anywhere in the world, no matter the time of day, without worrying about borders, public holidays or local jurisdictions.
- The lack of a central authority and the involvement of users in the security of the network keep you, as a user, in control of your own transactions.
- You can make payments without your personal information being tied to a transactions or passed on to the vendor or anyone else. This serves as a protection against

identity theft for a consumer and against fraud for a merchant.

- The Bitcoin blockchain is transparent and can be verified by anybody, but can't be manipulated by any person – or any government or organization.
- The fees associated with a payment are either non existent or very low, though they can be used to give a transaction more priority and thus speed it through the system.
- Bitcoin is a hot commodity right now and destined to remain so for a while. News at the end of 2017 that the currency had skyrocketed in value by a factor of tens of thousands brought an extreme amount of attention to it as an investment opportunity.
- Bitcoin is more liquid than any other cryptocurrency at this moment.
- It's replacing gold as the go to option for a safe haven for your wealth. This is because its quantity is fixed by math and also because of the lack of government interference.
- Bitcoin and other cryptocurrencies are allowing people around the world to access the traditional exchange systems that have never before had a way to do so. Estimates suggest that between a quarter and a third of the

planet's population have access to the internet, but lack access to exchange systems, and with this new cryptocurrency market the door has been opened for them.

- Bitcoin is available to anybody, no matter who or where you are. That's more important than it seems: consider, for example, those people who are regularly denied credit cards due to financial issues in their past, or countries in which legislation prevents certain groups of the population (often women) from having control over their own finances.

Cons

- There is still widespread ignorance about cryptocurrencies in general and Bitcoin in particular. The most notable effect of this is that it is not yet a widespread tool used in people's everyday lives and thus is still a niche currency. It is still relatively difficult to find vendors willing to accept it, for example.
- Because there is a limited amount of coins available and the attention Bitcoin is receiving causes demand to fluctuate wildly, the currency is exceptionally volatile at this time. This may well decrease as time goes on and awareness spreads, but for the near future it

will mean price jumps on a daily basis, often linked to news stories about Bitcoin and events related to cryptocurrencies around the world, such as new sanctions from individual governments.

- Bitcoin is still very new, compared to other currencies in use around the world, and that means it still contains flaws and unfinished features. For the forseeable future, it will remain a work in progress.
- A bitcoin is not actually a real thing. It's simply an algorithm developed by mathematics, rather than something you will ever be able to hold in your hands. Though a lot of people do grasp the idea that value is relative and depends entirely on what we decide it is, the idea of having to trust in an ephemeral entity is off putting to many.
- The use of Bitcoin and other cryptocurrencies in the recent past (and, in all honesty, probably at this moment) for illegal activities is not just off putting for a lot of people, it also brings extra scrutiny to the system, as a lot of people believe that Bitcoin is appealing in the first place because it can be used anonymously and thus can be taken advantage of for money laundering and other clandestine acts. In 2013,

Bitcoin was famously involved in the closure of the Silk Road website by the FBI, with an estimated $28 million worth of bitcoins seized that had been used to trade in drugs, guns and assassins.

- Combine this potential for illegal activity with the fact that a lot of individuals involved in the decision making for countries are not completely knowledgeable about cryptocurrencies and you have the potential for ongoing legislation for or against Bitcoin and its peers that constantly changes the playing field.
- There is a lack of security in Bitcoin that means there is no established and perfectly secure way to keep your bitcoins from certain pitfalls. These include human error, glitches in the system and fraud.
- Because the system was designed in the first place to limit how quickly transactions can take place and how many of them can be in progress, cryptocurrencies are not likely to replace money, debit cards and credit cards as a payment system any time soon, ensuring they remain niche.
- There is, and will always be, the possibility that the success of Bitcoin and other similar

currencies are experiencing an economic bubble. In such a situation, an asset is over valued and its price increases based purely on the speculation of its investors – their belief that it *will* increase in value. It depends which expert you ask as to how likely this is as opinions differ wildly across the board. Because cryptocurrencies are so new, any predictions about their future are based on older systems and experiences that may not be directly relatable. In other words, nobody can know for sure what will happen to the value of a bitcoin in the future.

The Principles of Bitcoin Investment

Having read that list of pros and cons, you are now in a position to make a more informed decision about your personal desire to invest in Bitcoin. If you're still reading, you probably still have an interest in doing so. In the next chapter, we will be entering the world of cryptocurrencies with your first Bitcoin wallet, but let's first prepare the ground with some general advice for investors at this stage of the technology's lifecycle.

As we've already discussed, cryptocurrencies have only emerged on the global scene recently and things are changing often and quickly – and sometimes bafflingly for the user who did not come prepared. As yet, there is no such thing as a conventional way of investing in cryptocurrencies – but there are some pearls of wisdom that can help you choose the best paths.

- Ignore temptation. The biggest issue you will face with cryptocurrency investment is fear. The sheer volatility of the market at this point in time can lead you to make rash decisions to either invest quickly and big before you miss out on a golden opportunity or get out of an investment in case it crashes beyond repair. This market is arguably more prone to causing investor fear than any other in existence simply because of its newness. However, as a new investor, it's important to follow the same principles you would in any other type of investment, especially to be conservative in the percentage of your available funds you are working with – and prepared to lose – at any one time.

- Think long term. If you are already an investor in other markets, this principle is familiar to you. Bitcoin and its fellows are new and exciting systems that have not yet had chance to settle down into a predictable pattern, which means their value can rocket skywards or plummet in the space of a day. When you make investments in the long term, you protect yourself from these daily ups and downs because all that matters to you is the general trend over time.

- Do your research. With all that said, how do you make long term investments in a system that is only marginally understood by the majority of mankind? To be a Bitcoin investor, you must be prepared to do deep research on any potential project, including the people involved and the product itself. Check that the demand is truly there for this project and that it will not be pipped to the post by a competitor and lost its potential gains. Ensure that the developers have the commitment, resources, knowledge and skill to actually bring their plans to fruition.

- **Always make sure you and your assets are protected**, no matter how safe you are told a transaction or system may be. There is no such thing as "unhackable", if a person out there really wants to find a way and is undeterred by the cost. Bitcoin and its peers simply haven't been around for long enough for every weak spot to have been tested and patched, particularly when third parties are involved. Bear in mind also that there is no central authority, which means there is no backup for any losses, which means you can lose your hard earned pennies just as easily and with the same finality as you would lose the cash in your wallet to a mugger on the street. The two golden rules for self protection in this fledgling world are: use a "soft" wallet protected by a set of codes and keys that works a lot like cloud storage. Transfer your currencies to an offline device once you have earned them, rather than leave them floating in cyberspace and vulnerable.

- **Watch out for fees.** For an investor, every penny matters. We've already mentioned that cryptocurrency transactions have the advantage of small or non existent fees in themselves, but that doesn't mean that an exchange can't tack fees on themselves for a potential investor. In this type of investment, even a tiny increase in fees can mean the difference between a return on your money or not, because of compounding interest on a long term project. Do your research when choosing an exchange and make sure that the combined price of the coins and the fees is acceptable to your long term plans.

Risk Reduction

As well as being often unpredictable and highly volatile, cryptocurrencies also represent a high risk compared to other types of investment. Of course, that also means you are working with a high potential return, so there's a plus side that makes it more than worthwhile to plunge right in.

So what kind of risks are you actually looking at in this market? Let's take a look.

- The volatility of digital currencies is slowly reducing over time, but it's still very much in existence and that is not likely to change in the near future. Thanks to breaking news on everything from daily drops and increases in the price to rumors about government action that will cause problems for cryptocurrency's growth as an entity, the market changes on a dime almost every day – and those changes are more dramatic than you will generally see in more traditional markets. You can offset this risk by making sure that the portfolio you build is diverse and does not focus entirely on one type of currency. Start with Bitcoin, but as you develop your portfolio, add in some of the other types of digital currency too.

- The risk of new regulations is one of the biggest fears of cryptocurrency investors. Individual countries are paying more and more attention to this new technology all the time and figuring out how to minimize its negative impact on their governmental operations and citizens. This means that you'll hear news about new regulations all the time, some more impactful than others. There is even a constant risk that governments will decide to outright ban the use of cryptocurrencies and this could be devastating for your investments. It's vital to keep one eye on the news at all times to follow the actions of governments around the world and prepare yourself for any decisions that could scupper your portfolio.

- As already mentioned in the chapter about pros and cons, there are still flaws in this young system that have yet to be worked out and there hasn't been time to figure out every possible weakness. Make sure that you, as the user, are always doing everything possible to protect your own assets and storing your money offline in a hard wallet, safe from harm.

Your First Bitcoins – and What to Put Them In

Ready to take the first steps and enter the world of cryptocurrencies? For that, you are going to need a bitcoin or two of your own and something to put them in.

To deal with cryptocurrency, you will need a wallet as a depository for your coins and a place for payments to start and end. There are several different types and you'll need to make a decision as to which one best suits you.

Every type, however, has a private key and a public key associated with it. The former is just for you and it should be guarded from any other eyes – you will be using it to sign all your transactions and authorizing the use of your assets so, obviously, you don't want anyone else knowing what it is and using it themselves.

The public key can be used to transfer money to you, much like giving someone your PayPal address. You can share this with anyone and everyone as all it allows them to do is give you money – it does not allow them to spend the money in your wallet.

It's also important to know that your wallet isn't actually, technically storing your Bitcoins – it's not a direct analogy to the wallet you keep in your pocket or purse. The coins are stored on the blockchain; the wallet just provides you with access to them by keeping hold of the keys you need.

There are two basic types of wallet:

- Cold Wallet – this type is not connected to the internet and thus cannot be accessed remotely, preventing hacking attempts. This is used for storing large amounts of currency that you do not intend to use at this moment.
- Hot Wallet – this is much like a checking account in that it's directly connected to the internet and the funds contained within can be spent right this minute using your key. They are considered to be hackable and most investors will only keep small amounts of currency in them for this reason.

You will find yourself faced with numerous choices when you look for the wallet you'd like to work with. You will need to think about the computer platform that best suits you, including what operating system it uses and whether it is a desktop computer or a mobile device like a cell phone or pad. You will also need to decide whether you want your platform to be based on your device or in the cloud, the latter being easier to set up but less secure.

Wallets on your device, for the most part, will include plenty of features and have better security. However, everything depends on keeping your device safe, so you are vulnerable to such things as accidentally dropping your cell phone in the bath or getting your iPad stolen.

If you decide a web based wallet is the better choice, be aware that they are more often targeted by hackers and you should select based on reputation and reviews, as well as a thorough examination of the security features. Web wallets are considered more convenient, but on the other hand you will not always be given access to the private key and you are under the control of the issuer.

There are numerous wallets available, so how do you choose? It's beyond the scope of this book to give detailed information on every single one, so head over to the Bitcoin web page and look at some of the most common options for yourself.

Some of the most common choices include:

- The first and original wallet is the Bitcoin Core, for example, which is the only one officially supported and also supports the Bitcoin network itself by storing the whole database on your computer. Unfortunately, it also has its downsides to offset the stability and security it offers. For instance, it has fewer features than other wallets and it can take up huge amounts of space and memory on your device thanks to the sheer volume of data that must be synced.

- ArcWare is designed for simplicity while allowing you full control over your money and comes with its own cold wallet storage feature with the ability to authorize a payment offline. As it can be loaded onto your pc, it can be vulnerable to malware.

- Blockchain has a great reputation and is quick and easy to set up, while guaranteeing good safety for your coins. However, as a web based option, it comes with the downsides associated with that type of wallet.

- mSigna boasts of having enterprise-level scalability and strong security, supporting such features as multi signature transactions, offline storage and synchronization across devices. However, it does not provide fee suggestions, which means your transactions can be delayed if the suggested fee is too low and you are not protected from high fees.

- Bither is available for multiple platforms and operating systems and has unique cold/hot modes built into it. However, its privacy is weak, which makes it easy for someone to look at your balance and payments because the same addresses are reused, and some information will be disclosed to your peers.

- Ledger is a cold storage option that uses a USB drive and has been designed with safety as its key. It can be used with any computer and is relatively easy to use.

- Trezor is another cold storage wallet type that always remains offline but is renowned for its flexibility and connectivity when you want to trade. Many see it as the most secure storage option available and like the fact that it is compatible with most computers and portable devices.

These are just a few of the options out there. More are added all the time, which makes it vital for you to do your research while bearing in mind your own unique circumstances. The more you intend to invest, the more security you will want – and the more important it is that you keep the majority of your assets in a cold storage wallet. The more trading you intend to do, the more you will want to protect yourself from prying eyes and ensure that your wallets are easy to understand and make use of.

You should also be aware that there is such a thing out there in the cryptocurrency jargon as a "paper wallet". This is as basic as it gets: it involves writing down your keys and addresses on paper and storing them somewhere safe. The huge disadvantage to doing this is that a piece of paper is easily lost or stolen. It's up to you whether you feel that you can keep information of that sort secure enough, but it's not necessarily to be recommended.

Whichever hot wallet option you choose, be aware that you are never going to be entirely free from risk. Be sure to take steps to keep yourself as protected as possible: don't store everything in one place, because it can be taken all at once, and keep separate email accounts for each of your wallets. And, one last time:

make sure you are keeping the vast majority of your assets offline.

Your Bitcoin Address

As we've mentioned previously, trading in Bitcoin requires a Bitcoin address, which is one of the first things you'll want to figure out once you've chosen your wallet or wallets.

Like email addresses, these Bitcoin addresses are unique to you and your wallet and can be used to communicate with you. Unlike email addresses, however, a Bitcoin wallet can actually have multiple addresses and it's even possible to create a unique one for every transaction you make.

Bitcoin addresses are between 26 and 35 characters in length and always begin either with a 1 or 3. They are case sensitive and must be entered absolutely correctly, or the transaction will fail.

Should you stick to a single address or create a new one for every transaction? Most experts agree that the latter option is best, mostly because repeatedly using the same address means losing a chunk of your anonymity.

Essentially, when you use an address, your actions are entered into the public ledger and become available for anyone to see, should they so wish. If the same address is linked to multiple transactions, an interested party will be able to see that, too.

Individual addresses can also be used in your own accounting to identify your transactions and keep records, as you will always be able to link your actions to specific addresses. If you are a business or you aim to trade with multiple individuals or customers, you can also create addresses to use with those contacts (but bear in mind you'll lose a little of the anonymity advantage by doing that).

The only reason not to use a new address each time is the fact that you'll have to actually create one. It doesn't take long and it's not difficult, but it is an added step.

In most cases, in fact, it's as simple as opening your wallet and clicking on the "Create New Address" button.

Finding Your First Coins

You have your infrastructure, now you need your coins. Because it's so new and thanks to its structure, you can't simply wander into the supermarket and add some to your trolley – you can't even go to a currency exchange kiosk and hand over your cash in exchange for coins.

Instead, you will need to use the most convenient method available to you, in your location and circumstances, to locate and purchase your first coins.

One thing you should definitely keep in mind before you do is that you cannot reverse a Bitcoin transaction. As soon as you hit that button, the transaction is final. Unfortunately, this introduces an element of risk for the person selling you the coins, as there is a possibility you could reverse your traditional payment – whether that be credit card, debit card, transfer or something else – as soon as you receive your coins, leaving the seller with nothing.

Because of this, most companies that do accept Bitcoin at this time will insist that you are verified and credit checked before they will trade with you. This can take a long time.

In the meantime, there are a few available methods to you for getting your hands on some coins. You could, for example, choose to trade with an acquaintance who has already entered the world of cryptocurrencies or use meetup.com to locate a meeting of users in your area. You can sell a product or service using cryptocurrencies as your payment method or find a classified service such as bitcointrading.com to find others in your area who are selling or trading in coins. You can also choose to use an exchange, which we'll cover in more detail in the next chapter.

Acquiring Coins

When you buy milk from a store, you hand over a bank note knowing exactly what it's worth and having decided, using that knowledge, that the product is fairly priced. Things are a little more difficult with coins because their worth fluctuates dramatically and quickly and because they are so new that few people can instinctively evaluate their worth.

However, the price of Bitcoin and other cryptocurrencies is still set by the market, just like any other type of currency. The supply and demand for coins in the various markets determines how much they are considered to be worth. You'll want to look at the market in your own area because, for instance, the price of Bitcoin in euros is calculated by looking specifically at how many Bitcoins have been bought and sold for euros, while the price in U.S. dollars reflects how many have been bought and sold with American currency.

You'll find a high number of websites that list the current market rate. It fluctuates by the second, so you should always check the exact rate just before agreeing to any transaction.

When you're ready to make your first trade and you've agreed on a price and amount with the seller, one way to go about this is to simply open your hot wallet, create a new address for yourself, enter the destination address for that seller and select how much to send either in cryptocurrency or your own local currency. You can also make your payment using traditional payment forms such as cash or a credit card.

The seller will use the address you have provided for them and send the amount of coins you have agreed on to your wallet. He or she will conclude the transaction and the network will be informed that it has been authorized. It will propagate across the network, where your wallet will notice it because it is constantly watching for any published transaction that match your address or addresses.

Just a few seconds after the seller hits the button, your wallet will indicate you have received your first coins. At first, it will be listed as unconfirmed, because the transaction has not yet been included in a block and added to the chain. This takes place approximately every ten minutes, which is thus how long it takes for a transaction to clear.

Bitcoin Exchanges

One of the most obvious things you can do with your Bitcoin and other cryptocurrencies is exchange it. In other words, you can buy or sell coins in exchange either for traditional currencies such as dollars or yen, or even for a different cryptocurrency.

You'll quickly notice, however, that there are myriad exchanges available out there – so which one do you choose? Let's take a look at some of the most popular and trustworthy.

- Coinbase – This exchange is only supported in 33 countries so you'll want to check to make sure yours – and any you are interested in trading within – are listed. It has a very high reputation in the cryptocurrency world and allows payments using wire or credit. Its transaction fees are considered to be low, but users note that its support department is not quick to respond to enquiries.

- CoinMama – This exchange operates worldwide and has a good reputation, with speedy transactions and a user interface that many consider to be friendly and easy to use.

However, be aware that its exchange rate is relatively high and some U.S. states do not allow its use.

- CEX.IO – Another exchange only available in a limited number of countries, CEX.IO has a great reputation and high buying limits but is also known for higher exchange rates than average. You can buy coins on this exchange for U.S. dollars, euros or rubles.

- Bitstamp – The oldest exchange still functioning, Bitstamp was established in 2011 and has the strong levels of respect associated with that success you might expect. Its transaction fees are low but, unfortunately, its user interface is among the most confusing out there and the payment methods you can use are limited.

- Bitfinex – Best used by experienced traders, this exchange is based in Hong Kong and has to be funded through altcoins or bitcoins. It has high liquidity and flexibility, but it does not accept flat deposits and its interface, again, is rather complicated.

- Bittrex – A little different to the others on this list in that it is known as the altcoin exchange and focuses on the new cryptocurrencies that appear on the market.

- Coinhouse – Based in Paris, you can buy coins for this exchange using prepaid cards called Neosurf that are available throughout Europe. However, this exchange can only be used in the Eurozone and has relatively high exchange rates. Its reputation, on the other hand, is solid.

- Bitpanda – An Austrian company, you can use multiple types of payment on this exchange and the fees are relatively low. On the other hand, it only supplies service to European countries and its fees are hidden inside the exchange rate.

- Gemini – This exchange has public owners – Tyler and Cameron Winklevoss – and is regarded as one of the most trustworthy exchanges in existence. The pair work with regulators to lead the way in attempting to conform with local legislations, primarily in the United States. Its downside is that it only supports a limited number of currencies at this time and that it is not yet a leader in the market.

- GDAX – This exchange is the "sister" to Coinbase and works with it closely, with users on Coinbase able to use the same account details for GDAX. It does not, however, support altcoins, though it does have low fees and supports ether and litecoins.

- Kraken – Another name that commands respect in the industry, Kraken is known for being reliable and for its low fees. On the other hand, it has the disadvantages of a difficult to navigate interface, a low number of payment methods available and high deposit fees on small transactions.

That's a long list of exchanges, but barely scratches the surface. The good news for you is that there is almost certainly one out there that suits your specific needs and tastes – you may simply need to shop around a little bit to find it.

It's obviously a very good idea to do your research before settling on a choice of exchange, and not just in terms of suiting your currency, interface and payment needs. There are new exchanges popping up all the time and not all of them are as reliable as they may claim, so make sure to seek out reviews of you shortlist and find out how trustworthy they are thought to be and whether there are any hidden downsides that you might regret later.

Some tips for registering on an exchange once you have made your selection:

- Turn on two factor authentication, an additional layer of security that will ensure only you can access your account, even if somebody else discovers your password. If you're not familiar with the term, don't worry – you probably use it all the time without knowing it. For instance, your online banking system might ask you to answer a security question when you log on, as well as enter your username and password. Two factor authentication, as in that example, works on the basis of "what you have AND what you know"; you HAVE a password, and you KNOW the name of your favorite teacher in elementary school.

- Choose the strongest password you can. It should include a mixture of upper case letter, lower case letters and digits. Make sure it is entirely unique and is not used on any other exchanges or any other personal accounts.

- Use two different exchanges at a minimum. The world of cryptocurrencies is fast paced and constantly changing, so there will always be a risk of something happening to one of your exchanges. By having two or even three available to you, this won't prevent you from closing the orders you want to close.

- Remember to always move your profits into your cold wallet – only ever store the bare minimum of currency on the exchanges you have selected. Though the risk is still relatively low, hackers could steal your money at any time.

You can, of course, also sell your coins on these exchanges. Many people rely on arranging meet ups with other people in person to make exchanges of coins but this does come with the physical risks you would expect – as in many cases you do not know the person, they could be planning to threaten or harm you to take those coins rather than pay for them. You can also sell your coins by using them for a purchase, finding a vendor that accepts cryptocurrency.

But an exchange is probably the easiest way. Using an exchange, you can buy the coins you want and also sell them, which you may choose to do if the exchange rate is particularly favorable and you want to cash out on your holdings, or if you were using Bitcoin to save for a purchase.

When you sell through an exchange, you sell to the exchange, rather than to another individual. Check whether your exchange of choice allows you to do this and always remember that the exchange is there to make money, so it may short change you more than you're willing to be short changed.

The best way to mitigate that is, of course, to shop around – check a number of different exchanges and see how much you would get at each one. Compare this to the in person possibilities in your area. When you are happy that you have found the best option, go ahead and sell your coins.

Spending Digital Coins

A quick note before we move on: though it is still relatively rare, there are a growing number of establishments around the world that will accept crpytocurrencies as a form of payment. Do a little research to find out if there are any retail establishments in your area accepting Bitcoin at their points of sale – depending on your area, there may be a few.

For instance, some airports are letting you pay for your parking with coins. State governments in the U.S. are looking at allowing citizens to pay their bills using cryptocurrencies. The available outlets might just surprise you, so keep an eye out for what and where you can spend your coins.

Online retailers may be an even better choice for you, especially if you live in a rural area. Overstock.com was the first big retailer to accept coins in 2014 and, through that site, you can purchase plenty of furnishings, electronics and more.

Other options at the present time include booking a vacation through Expedia, purchasing gift cards through eGifter, buying gadgets and electronics at Newegg, purchasing from individual sellers at

Shopify or paying for your television subscription with Dish.

You can even buy a pizza with your digital currency through PizzaForCoins or buy your games and movie streaming downloads through Microsoft. The possibilities grow constantly.

All you need to be able to make a purchase, online or in the physical world, is your wallet and some coins to put in it. It works at the point of sale by automatically converting the total price from the local currency, such as the euro or Canadian dollar, into bitcoins at the prevailing market rate. For the vendor, the price will be displayed in both currencies.

The point of sale system will then create a QR code – the square symbol that resembles a barcode but with dots instead of lines, which you can scan with your phone to retrieve information. In this case, the code contains the relevant information about where the payment needs to go and a request for that payment, as well as the amount.

You, as the customer, can then scan that code and see the payment, pressing the button to authorize the payment. Within a matter of seconds, the vendor will see that the transaction is complete and your purchase will be complete.

Using coins in the real world is as simple as that – although, of course, it could be a very long time before your local supermarket, gas station and cafe are willing to take the plunge and join the digital revolution, so you'll have to pick and choose your purchases for now if using coins for payments is one of your goals.

Of course, you can always sidestep that downside. You could consider investing in a cryptocurrency debit card, which functions exactly the same way as a regular debit card except that it is connected to your Bitcoin wallet. For instance, CryptoPay is one of the oldest available and will offer you either a chip or a PIN card that can be used anywhere that a Visa card is normally accepted.

Coinbase also offers a debit card with an excellent reputation, removing the funds from your Bitcoin wallet to match the dollar value of what you are buying. These two are probably the ones with the best reputation in the business but, again, a little research into the most current available options will go a long way.

Investing in Bitcoin

Buying cryptocurrency is one way of making your digital wallet a little heavier, but it's not the only possibility. There are, in fact, a few ways through which you can earn some coins of your own that you can then use to trade later.

One of the most common ways to make money in the cryptocurrency arena is through investments. In the old days, a lot of people opted to invest their money through stocks, shares or even a retirement fund, putting their money aside in such a way that they can retrieve it later along with the extra it has made for them during that time.

Nowadays, the rise of cryptocurrencies and the innovations that have sprung up alongside have made the digital environment ripe for investment, too. In the long term, some suggest it might even prove to be a more fruitful place to put your money.

Long Term Investments

Bitcoin and its peers have advantages over the usual long term investments people make, such as gold, real estate or stocks and shares. In particular, its value has gone from mere cents to thousands of dollars and that kind of rise is unlikely to stop, even though it will inevitably slow down.

For many, though, there is a lingering anxiety that the rise must stop eventually – and may be followed by a dramatic crash. This worry seems to be supported by the rises and falls that happen on a daily basis.

But let's not forget that this technology is new. We have only just begun to explore the possibilities of cryptocurrencies and the blockchain technology underneath them. In the previous chapter, we discussed all the different places you can already spend your coins, and that spread is almost certainly going to continue.

True, digital coins are not as stalwart as gold and don't have the test of time to stand on. However, many experts believe that the market will grow to ten times its current size in just the next few years – and it's impossible to know what heights it might rise to from there.

The key to investing in Bitcoin and other cryptocurrencies is going to be in holding the line. When you invest long term, you are interested only in the big picture: the continuous rise over time, rather than the dips and climbs that the graph shows when you zoom in much closer.

Those dips and climbs happen in response to what's going on in the world. We've already discussed the impacts of world events such as government legislation, investment from large companies, criminal use of the system and even basic news stories about the pros and cons of cryptocurrencies. These tend to lead to moments where investors either buy big, driving up the price, or back away and sell, driving it down.

Despite these rises and falls, Bitcoin seems set to continue rising in price overall for the foreseeable future. Combine this with the additional advantage that Bitcoin is a currency in itself. You can't spend a stock, but you can spend your coins, so you can use your investment at any time on necessary purchases.

This also means that simply owning your Bitcoin (or other currencies, should you wish to diversify) counts as an investment – that's really all you have to do. The longer you hold on to it and the less you give in to anxiety when bad press hits, the more you are likely to make from your investment when the time comes to cash out.

Short Term Trading

If you are an experienced investor, short term trading with cryptocurrencies is worth considering. As a beginner, it may require more research into the basics of short term trading and it would likely be worth dipping your toes into more traditional markets before turning your attention to digital currencies.

Essentially, a short term trader attempts to purchase coins at a low price and sell them at a higher price, repeating the process over and again to make profits along the way that stack into a worthwhile chunk of cash. In traditional stocks, this tends to be done in conjunction with major events in the world that are likely to impact the entity associated with the stock. The same is now happening with Bitcoin.

It works, for the most part, because Bitcoin is a volatile thing. Its value can jump up and down through several percent in a single day – and that's just a normal day, without the influence of the news stories, political interventions and other happenings we've already discussed.

It also works for the savvy investor by taking a look at alternative cryptocurrencies, or altcoins. As we mentioned earlier, there are a lot of different options out there and new ones can appear at any time, which typically attract a lot of attention before disappearing when investors grow tired of them. The upswing doesn't last long, but there is profit to be made in the short time the currency is favored for.

Whether or not you feel that short term investments are worthwhile will largely depend on your opinion towards Bitcoin as a currency. Because it is not backed by gold or any other item, and there is no regulation, it is supremely volatile and its moods can be dramatic.

It also isn't traded on Wall Street, which means you will need to do the bulk of the work yourself and will likely need to keep up with your research and knowledge of current events more closely than you would with traditional investments.

However, it's global, it's always available to trade no matter the time of day and its volatility can be incredibly profitable for the savvy investor. It's also great for individual investors because if can be traded with leverage, using platforms such as Plus500 to generate returns beyond your initial investment.

It's also relatively insulated from local risks thanks to its independence; only developments that specifically affect Bitcoin and its peers will generally have an impact on its price. This can reduce the amount of research and prediction you need to do to make educated guesses about price swings.

Investing in Companies

One thing it's vital to be aware of when thinking about Bitcoin investments is that we are essentially dealing with a new wild west here. You will undoubtedly come across numerous sites and companies that claim they can double your coins, provide you with interest daily or similar if you invest in their scheme – the best advice to follow in these cases is to avoid like the plague.

What some of these companies are doing is essentially bringing together a group of investors, using your money to try their money making strategy. It may or may not work and it probably won't, to put it politely.

Others are, purely and simply, scamming you out of your money. In a lot of recorded cases, the company will take your money, pay your returns for a while and generate excitement through this perceived success. They'll introduce you to a referral program, encouraging you to bring in others, and the buzz around them will grow. Then, a few months later, they will simply disappear – you'll never get another payment and it's unlikely you'll have received enough from your payments to cover your initial investment.

In general, the golden rule is to stay away from any offer that claims it can double your investment or give you payments daily on your investment. It's almost a given that they can't. If in any doubt whatsoever, steer clear and don't look back.

Your Investment Strategy

Should you invest or shouldn't you? Is long term better than short term? Unfortunately, in this fledgling environment, there is no hard and fast answers to this question.

In the next chapter, we'll go into more detail about short term trading using traditional methods. For now, feel free to table this question until you reach the end of this book, have done a little research in specific areas that interested and have dipped your toes into the cryptocurrency waters.

Whatever you decide, bear in mind that digital currencies are uncharted waters even now and there is no advice an expert can give you that will help you make a decision. Never invest more than you can afford and, if in doubt, don't invest at all – and don't forget that by simply owning Bitcoins, you are already investing in your future.

Contracts for Differences – New Trading, Old Rules

There is, as strange as it may sound, a way to trade in Bitcoin without actually owning any Bitcoin. Contracts for Differences (CFDs) were invented in the first place to allow traders to expose themselves to Bitcoin without having to actually buy any.

A CFD is a contract between a trader and an exchange, which declares that the difference between that trader's entry and exit price will be their profit or loss. It's an agreement between two parties that simulates the actual Bitcoin being owned by the trader.

You can use it to go long, betting that the price of Bitcoin will rise, or to go short, betting that its price is going to fall. You can take advantage of the always open cryptocurrency market by opening trades whenever you like and closing them with similar flexibility. The fees are lower than most other markets, though slightly higher than for simply buying Bitcoin directly.

They're seldom used for long term investments because there is a premium for keeping them open, which will eat a small percentage of your position every day. Interest must be charged while the CFD is open, which is not something you must face when simply storing your coins in a wallet.

It's also worth bearing in mind that the exchange you use will also be aiming to protect itself from the downsides of market volatility. Every so often, the market will move so drastically that your position could easily place your balance a long way into the red; if you can't cover that loss, the exchange faces a loss itself – some have gone bankrupt through just such a situation.

For this reason, your trades will include a margin call in which your trade will be automatically closed out before your balance goes into the negative. The more funding you have available, the less likely this is, but it's always a possibility.

You can think of it as a protection in some ways – the exchange will prevent you from suffering such a giant loss that your bank balance will never recover and you needn't even ask them to make that happen. On the other hand, the volatility of the market means that such a giant dip is often followed by an even more enormous climb. Because your position was closed out, you were cut out of the equation before that climb had a chance to happen.

Many of the big names in CFD trading, such as Avatrade or Plus500, will allow you to download a demo version of the software so that you can have a go at trading without actually risking any of your cash. If the idea of CFDs interests you, consider spending some time playing with one of these demos so that you can see for yourself how the trading will unfold and how well it suits you.

In fact, it's a good idea to stay with the demo until you've figured out a personal strategy that is reaping demonstrable profits on a consistent basis, especially if you are new to trading altogether. If you are a seasoned trader, it can still help to use the demo mode to become familiar with the unique properties of Bitcoin in trading.

When you're ready, you can use a range of different credit and debit cards to fund your account, as well as PayPal. You can then make your first CFD purchase. Bear in mind at this moment that the buy price is always going to be higher than the sell price so you will always be starting at a loss. In other words, if you hit buy and then sell immediately after one another, you'd get back less money than you put in because it cost you more to buy than you got from selling.

You'll then need to learn how to read the price of coins over time. This is done through candlesticks on most charts, which are colored blocks that are usually colored green if indicating upwards movement and red if indicating downwards movement.

Many apps also feature inbuilt price charts that allow you to see the movement of prices over time. As with most stocks and shares, experts grow able to make relatively accurate predictions over time, which you can largely achieve through studying the chart in comparison to the incoming news about Bitcoin and its peers. You can usually customize your charts and even annotate them, adding your own notes about what was taking place when the currency grew or fell.

Generally, you'll trade in CFDs in one of a few days, depending on your own preferences:

- You can buy currency to keep hold of, attempting to accumulate as much of it as you can over time with the idea that it will increase in value and will eventually become extremely valuable. When you're dealing with a commodity like Bitcoin, the basis of this strategy is in the fact that there is only a limited amount available – and there always will be a limit. The day to day movement of the currency won't bother you too much as you will be thinking in terms of what coins will be worth weeks, months or years from now. However, while this is a great strategy for Bitcoin, it doesn't translate well to CFDs due to the premium, which accumulates over time and ultimately will negate the profits you are likely to make.

- You can become a day trader, watching the prices fluctuate over the course of a single working day and closing out trades during that time, making small amounts of profit at a time but on a regular basis. This works well for CFDs, except during times when the market is not very volatile. (Note that CFDs don't fit very well with extremely short periods – trading on minute to minute movement is not generally profitable).

- You can watch for trends that occur on a relatively long term basis – weeks and months, rather than minute to minute. You are looking for the peaks and troughs in the price chart, buying and selling at those moments (if, of course, you are able to catch them correctly) to make the most profit. This strategy works well for traders who are able to predict when the market is about to swing in the opposite direction because, for example, a news story has caused a number of people to sell out of their currency or because an abundance of purchases has unbalanced the market.

- You can watch for long trends with the aim of riding them as long as they last. In this case, you would buy in at a moment when the currency is relatively low and sell when you believe the upswing is coming to an end, just in time to make maximum profits. This must generally be done over days and weeks and requires a keen eye and great timing – if it interests you, it can be helpful to use that demo mode to your advantage to learn the market trends.

How can you become a better trader and learn to spot those trends that can make you a profit through CFDs? Largely by understanding the fundamental fact that trading is based on the fear of losing profit and the desire to gain it. The information that comes out in the news cycle will drive either one of these emotions – and it's up to you to predict which. The market also follows a "mood" of its own, sometimes continuing in the same direction despite a new data point that you would have thought was going to push it in the other. With time and attention, you will learn to spot this "mood" as well as the news and information that is likely to make an impact.

Becoming a Bitcoin Miner

All the way back at the beginning of this book, we mentioned that cryptocurrencies and the blockchain are underpinned by the participation of miners: computers that store the ledger and add to it, validating new transactions as they come in. As probably occurred to you when you read that, mining is indeed a way to enter the world of cryptocurrencies and make some cash by doing so.

As a Bitcoin miner, your job will be to verify other transactions – it's as simple as that. It's not even something you will need to do yourself; your computer will do all the work for you. All you need to do is make the computational power available for the network to use.

Computational Power

The downside, of course, is that the power you make available must be worth using, and the blockchain is a power hungry beast. You will need to invest in custom hardware capable of storing the ledger and participating in the process.

At first, when cryptocurrencies and blockchain technology were just becoming popular, this wasn't a problem. Most high end home computers had a CPU and GPU that could handle this. These days, however, your chances of making a profit by mining depend entirely on how much you are willing and able to spend on your hardware set up – and the electricity it will take to run it. You're going to need a specific piece of equipment that plugs into your computer like a sound or graphics card, which increases your processing power while keeping your electricity spend around the same. It's called an ASIC miner, a special computer that was built specifically for Bitcoin mining.

The amount of money you can make, you see, will depend how many operations your machine is able to complete every second, known as the "hash rate". Your performance will be measured in mega hash per second, giga hash per second or terra hash per second.

The cost for a machine will range from the hundreds of dollars to the tens of thousands, depending on the hash rate you are aiming to achieve. Bear in mind also that the machine will likely consume more electricity the more powerful it is and it's therefore advisable to research that cost before purchasing.

The available machines change almost by the day, so you'll need to research the most current to make your choice. Efficiency will be a big factor in that choice because you can literally wipe out the profits you are making with the electricity costs, if you're not careful.

The best way to figure out if your pc set up is going to help you make a profit through mining is by searching online for a "Bitcoin mining calculator", which will allow you to enter the details of the hardware you ware considering and will tell you, in return, how long it is going to take you to either break even or make a profit. Be warned that, as this field becomes more competitive as more people develop a curiosity about it, the more difficult it's going to become to even break even.

Getting Started

You're going to need a Bitcoin wallet to be a miner and an address to go along with it. Make sure, if you are using a self hosted wallet on your computer, that you keep a copy of the wallet.dat file on a USB drive and also print a copy out so that, if your computer fails, you haven't lost all your coins.

You are also going to need the software to mine, and again you'll find there are all sorts of options out there for you to choose from. A quick search will allow you to find and compare the most common and popular ones and you can choose according to your operating system and hardware and the trustworthiness according to reviews. Almost all software options are free and open source; bear in mind that your pool (more in the next section) may require you use a particular program.

Mining Pools

Now you'll want to find and join a mining pool. A group of miners who combine their computational power with the aim of making more coins. It's a bit like a syndicate grouping together to win the lottery: coins are awarded to miners in blocks of around 12.5 and a solo miner could wait forever to be the lucky recipient, while a pool has the combined power to be able to solve larger algorithms and earn coins based on that contribution.

When selecting a pool, ask how they share out the proceeds before joining and be sure that you agree with their methods. Ask if they charge any fees for joining and participating and how easy it will be for you to withdraw your portion of the coins. Research how stable the pool is – how long it has been running and how long its members have been around – and, of course, ask for a record of their successes in finding blocks and getting rewarded for doing so.

Again, a quick internet search will throw up many different mining pools for you to choose from based on the current selection that's out there. When you've chosen, you'll simply need to configure your machine to connect to the pool and launch the software – with that done, you've begun mining and you'll be paid for your share of the work when the pool is rewarded.

Initial Coin Offerings

Referred to as ICOs, Initial Coin Offerings are the cryptocurrency equivalent of an IPO, or Initial Public Offering. It's a way for you to get in early on the "next Bitcoin" and buy a little of that brand new currency before its value is recognized by the masses and starts to increase.

If you are at all familiar with stocks and shares, you will already know that this refers to the initial offering of stocks to the public and the fact that the people who agree to buy those stocks then become co-owners of that particular company. In return, the company gets the money from the sale of the stocks to invest in its operations and future.

Most businesses launch an IPO as a funding mechanism. It's perfectly legal and a great way to build up capital in the early days of building the company, though it's a long and somewhat expensive journey to make.

For the buyer, it's a risk, because the business is almost always very new and there is, of course, the possibility that it will not grow and thrive and the investment will be wasted. On the other hand, if you are canny enough to invest in the next big thing, the value of those stocks could continue to grow and grow and reap great rewards for you when it comes time to sell.

An ICO is a similar thing, only the commodity on offer is not shares in a new traditional business, but in a startup cryptocurrency venture that aims to create and launch a new project and requires capital to do it. You, as the investor, will be buying brand new coins from a brand new currency that could easily rise in value as the currency takes off and gains popularity.

It's an unregulated way of raising funds by which the backers of the project are sold a percentage of the new cryptocurrency in exchange for other coins or, sometimes, traditional currency. In most cases, the startup will put together a white paper describing the project and its aims, as well as the amount of money needed to complete it, how much of the proceeds will remain with the startup and how long the project will run for.

As an investor, in return for your money you will be issued "tokens", which are intended to become units of functional currency when the funding goal of the startup has been met and the project launches. It's basically a form of crowdfunding that allows new businesses to bypass the regulations that would normally apply to them and go straight to their potential investors. That's great but, as you can imagine, it also means there's a high level of risk for you involved.

It can be profitable if you are savvy in your investment choices, because a lot of people will withdraw their money as soon as they earn it back and thus the first coins will zoom up sharply and then drop as people begin to sell.

A startup that wants to launch an ICO is a startup that has an idea of the project it wants to pursue, but probably doesn't yet have a business plan or a minimum viable product. Their first move will be to conduct a pre-ICO, a token sale event that takes place before the crowdsale or campaign begin, usually done to raise money for marketing so that the startup can drum up more interest for its fundraising.

If the startup fails to raise enough money during the ICO campaign, all the money that has been raised is returned to the people who invested and the ICO is declared to have been unsuccessful. If enough money is made, on the other hand, it is then used to either begin the project or complete it.

Once again, ICOs are fledgling entities, relatively untested and ripe for abuse as they grow. In 2017,

China actually banned them, calling them disruptive to the stability of the country's finances and economy. Were they right? Time will tell, but the message that you should take away is that an ICO has the possibility of great returns, but should be approached with extreme caution.

At the present time, estimates suggest that under 4 percent of startups of this nature will actually survive. How can you be sure to put your money into this vanishingly small number of good investments? Mostly by investing for the right reasons – and not just that you believe in the product that this company is aiming to create.

Belief in the viability of the product is definitely a great starting point, but you should wait until the company begins trading so you can be sure that there is a future to their business. You should then be on the lookout for a set of characteristics that tends to set the good investments apart from the bad ones:

- The people running the project, particularly at high levels of the business, are easy to research and have been publically visible for some time before the business was announced.

- The aims and objectives of the project are clearly defined – you can see the end point, and you can see how the company intends to get there in acceptable detail.

- Any other companies in the same market are doing well and making profits, suggesting that the commodity the startup wants to offer will meet with demand.

- Others in the community of cryptocurrencies are supportive of the company and its members and have evaluated the startup plan in a positive light.

- "Coin talk" forums are talking about the new currency and have a positive opinion of it and how it will work.

- The company has been transparent in as many ways as possible, including in its descriptions of the product and its employees.

- The new currency will have value in the long term and will be useful to those who use it. To determine this, think about how this particular currency could provide a value to groups of people, organizations, industries and so on. It might be that it will provide a platform for other companies, in which case you might judge it has long term value as those companies use it as a foundation and continue to rely on it. It might provide additional value to a certain market and thus have long term possibilities.

- A red flag that some investors watch out for is the mention of mining very early on in the literature. This sometimes means that the project developers have no more significant feature to push to its investors, which is a bad sign because mining is just a part of how the currency will work and is not a feature.

- Check out BitcoinTalk.org, currently the most used forum for issues related to cryptocurrencies. Most startups will make an announcement here and you can tell a lot about the viability of the project by what they choose to say on this site. Look to see whether they have answered the questions and concerns of their potential investors – if they sidestep questions, that's almost always a red flag.

- Lean towards projects with hard caps on the amount of currency that will ultimately be made available. The more coins that end up in circulation, the less your own will be worth because the lower the demand will fall.

- Take a look at the code already written or ask a friend with experience of programming to do so. The quality of the code will tell you a lot about the attitude of the people who wrote it – if it's clean and well written, these are probably developers who believe in what they are doing.

- Read the white paper from start to finish and make notes about the pros and cons of the project. Ask yourself as you finish what this project is going to do for the world and whether you, as an investor, believe in it.

As and when you find an investment that you feel confident about, navigate to its website and find the page on which tokens are for sale. Buy as many tokens as you feel comfortable with and then simply wait.

How long should you wait for? That's up to you but, especially as a beginner and particularly with investments you are not entirely sure about, it's a good idea to exit as soon as you have made a conservative profit and then reinvest that money in a new ICO.

Lending Your Coins

We've covered some of the best, most popular and most obvious ways to make some money using cryptocurrencies, but there is another hiding in the background that a lot of people are unaware of completely, but has great possibilities as part of your overall strategy.

Loaning out the coins you have already made is a way to earn some cash using your cryptocurrency that requires very little effort from you but will provide you with constant, reliable returns. Just like a bank, you can lend out coins to other people and they will later pay you back along with the interest accrued.

The interest rates generally fluctuate according to the amount of risk involved in the loan – if you are given collateral in exchange, for example, the rates will be low but so will the risk to you. If there is no collateral or low collateral, the risks will be higher but so too will be the interest. Rates can also fluctuate according to the volatility of the overall market.

The big cryptocurrency names tend to have inbuilt systems for lending, though you'll also find entire currencies based on this purpose. Bitcoin, for example, has Unchained Capital, which allows investors to make loans against the collateral of bitcoins. Ethereum offers SALT, a platform that requires no credit checks and allows borrowing with SALT tokens as collateral.

To become a lender, you'll want to sign up for and use a lending exchange such as Poloniex, which acts as the middle man between people borrowing coins for their investments and the people from whom they are borrowing.

The amount you can make from lending will vary according to the currency you choose to lend, because each of them have their own interest rates and these will change according to supply and demand. Typically, you can expect a small return per day below 0.04 percent – which might sound very small, but that's because we're used to hearing about interest rates on an annual basis. Multiply that tiny gain by 365 and you'll realize how good the interest rates really can be.

Sometimes, if the volatility is particularly high, the interest rates can jump to high levels indeed – it's not unheard of for them to exceed 1 percent. This will generally happen a few times a year and you'll find that the price spikes arrive with "shorters" following right behind, intent on making a quick profit by buying low and selling high, so it's a great time for a lender.

Lending coins isn't going to make you a fortune, but it's a good idea to add it to your cryptocurrency portfolio nevertheless. Why? Because you can invest a portion of your available coins in a strategy that has a relatively low risk most of the time and that is mostly done on an automated basis. You'll be earning higher annual interest than you would if you loaned your money to a bank and you'll be doing so without the need to pay much attention to what the exchange is doing on your behalf.

The reason you shouldn't focus entirely on lending is that the returns you can expect will be smaller than with strategies such as investment. You should also avoid locking all your available funds into lending and thus making them unavailable when you see a trading or investment opportunity.

If you're concerned about possible losses when a borrower makes risky trades and ends up losing the coat from their back, rest assured that most exchanges are set up to protect you from that loss. Accounts that find themselves in irreversible levels of trouble are liquidated automatically and the balance used to pay back the loans the account owes.

The only time that you may find yourself unprotected is when the market is at its highest levels of volatility and the exchange simply can't keep up and get good enough prices to pay back the loans. This, however, happens extremely rarely.

So don't feel afraid to set aside a portion of your capital to lend out on the exchange. To do this, you can simply set up an account on the lending page of the exchange and transfer the funds you want to lend out into that account. You can now set up loan offers, choosing a competitive interest rate by looking at the list of other offers available at that moment. You can then also choose the duration: how long the borrower will have to pay you back.

When you're happy with your choices, you can also set up an auto renew, which will tell the exchange to create a new offer with the same terms when the first one is paid back. You can disable this at any time, but checking the box means the exchange will keep working on your behalf without your intervention.

Wondering how to make those choices in the first place? Here are a few tips to get you started:

- If you set your rate just a fraction below the one that's currently right at the bottom, you'll be near the top of the offer list and will thus attract more attention from borrowers that are looking right now for a loan.

- Choose your duration according to the current lending rates. A couple of days is usually a good time, because you'll have the money back within a short time frame and can change your settings if there's an upwards spike. On the other hand, if those rates are already higher than usual, you can extend your duration by several more days to take advantage of them.

- Check your accounts daily and make adjustments as you see results coming in. That way, you can make sure on a regular basis that all the money in your account is being put to use and that borrowers are actually taking advantage of your offers. Make sure you're setting up offers even when rates are low, because a small return is better than no return at all.

The Future of the Blockchain

It wasn't too long ago that an economist or financial expert would have had trouble giving you a positive review of the future of Bitcoin. Even now, with so many people still so unaware of the potential of the blockchain, we have still only just begun to explore the possibilities.

I mention this as we reach the end of the book because you, too, have only just begun your journey into the world of cryptocurrencies. We've covered some of the best ways for you to get involved right now and we've looked at the pros, cons and potential disasters you will encounter as you take that plunge into this brand new slice of human ingenuity.

Even now, you count as an early uptaker. You have still come into this world much sooner than the majority of your peers and you will be right there on hand when new possibilities present themselves.

The best advice I can give you at this moment is to explore all the ways to get involved in cryptocurrencies and make the most of them – but to always keep one eye trained firmly on the future. Keep reading those news stories, keep watching the forums, keep paying attention to all the innovations that are happening on a daily basis. By doing that, you will be among the first to take advantage of those innovations as they come along – and you'll be swept along in the next gold rush as you do.

And finally, a reminder to be cautious. At this time, cryptocurrencies are a long way from replacing traditional currencies, investments and trading. For the foreseeable future, a conservative strategy would be to divide your attention and available funds between the traditional avenues of stocks, shares, bonds and capital investments and the new avenues that have opened through the blockchain.

The future is coming, but it isn't yet quite here – it's a great time to get yourself involved in the journey. You can make a healthy amount of money right now through the possibilities of digital finance, but there will undoubtedly be even more ways to do so in the near future.

Ultimately, by making sensible, well researched investments in cryptocurrencies now, you will be perfectly positioned to welcome that future when it arrives – and you'll have a thicker, heavier wallet in your hand as you stand there waiting on the red carpet.

Special Thanks

I would like to give special thanks to all the readers from around the globe who chose to share their kind and encouraging words with me.

Knowing even just one person found this book helpful means the world to me.

If you've benefited from this book at all, I would be honored to have you share your thoughts on it, so that others would get something valuable out of this book too.

Your reviews are the fuel for my writing soul, and I'd be **<u>forever grateful</u>** to see *your* review, too.

Thank you all

www.ingramcontent.com/pod-product-compliance
Lightning Source LLC
Chambersburg PA
CBHW071721170526
45165CB00005B/2106